Tate's poetry is a stillness intimate with family, art, kinship of living, dying things; with the immediacy of sensual impressions that, as the mind moves on, linger, pulling it back, anchoring it; with the self at once solitary and connected through senses that touch on other worlds: bodies and cultures in dialog, but more than that—caressing, intertwining.

—DENI ELLIS BÉCHARD

The Silk the Moths Ignore chronicles both loss and joy in its peculiar, sensual language, all the while keeping its focus on the mind's movement as it tracks that which is beyond or below attention, a "sea so calm we do not note the tide," in "a language no known mother tongued." Here is a poet who ignores nothing, whose description brings us into the immersive space of experiences that are not ours, but are nonetheless felt fully. The lived and the linguistic find a common articulation in this work, given that the "tongue is word and taste"; this is an exhilarating and perceptive book which values, as does Hillary Gravendyk's own indelible work, the homes we make within both nature and language.

—JESSICA FISHER

In her magnificent debut collection, Bronwen Tate's rich textured language attends to the facets of her speaker's gleaming universe. Carefully collected images skitter across the page to illuminate the ache and intensity of mothering when the speaker's life revises this desire at every turn. In a voice of distilled triumphs and heartbreak she reminds the reader that rage and tenderness are of the same stardust, "Lace is made of holes." Through the germinal magic of tousled poppies and creation-spells, the speaker ultimately sows the "the beauty of beings" with clarity. Part experiment of form and heart, part testament to hidden, everyday joy, I keep close these poems that ponder the miracle of the overlooked world, to consider, indeed, "the silk the moths ignore."

—RAJIV MOHABIR

The Silk
The Moths Ignore

The Silk
The Moths Ignore

BRONWEN TATE

Inlandia Books

Copyright Information
The Silk the Moths Ignore
Copyright © 2021 by Bronwen Tate
ISBN: 978-1-7344977-7-9
Library of Congress Control Number: 2021932930

Cover art: Vesper Elinor Tate Anderson
Book design and layout: Kenji C. Liu

Printed and bound in the United States
Distributed by Ingram

Published by Inlandia Institute
Riverside, California
www.InlandiaInstitute.org
First Edition

for Owen and Vesper

CONTENTS

FOR THE COLORS
OF A NEW PLACE

White agate   goldenrod
now walk ahead
      hear daughter cry
shrill thread   I want to dye
all yellow

TO HEAR THE ECHO

Baby's
gripping fist
       drips melon
bathe her bare belly
sticky soft

*

When his tears subside
lower Owen
         into water
            softer
nape and tender spine

REPRODUCTIONS OF FRESCOS

Travel back. Because of a misstep, I saw a crevice in a horse's knee in place of brigands. Play of light and color off their helms. Reading in the original French. Reading to be elsewhere. I look past it, first conception.

I read Proust. In wide-sleeved houppelande, she incarnates. Swollen fruit of her manly form a solid allusion. Prod that membrane edged with ribbons of watercress or cuckoo flower.

For each word, a word in another language means part of the same thing. When I look up "midwife" on the university website, the only reference is to Plato. *Theaetetus*, he suggests, *is in discomfort because he is in intellectual labour.* Socratic Method, maieutics without a uterus, the skill of drawing thought from a latent mind.

I too want to be a scholar. I want a new vernacular of milk.

Echo, echo, on my perch with my library. Well-stocked dictionary sends me Latin, lygeum spartum, cultivated or not present here.

AND SO THE SAME EVENT SPREADS OPPOSING BRANCHES

Early vervaine tisane. A little bite dissolves. It's a beginning, bait.

Early expectation all potential waste. Poppy seed, blueberry, kumquat.

In the dark, a sundial says nothing. Opaque, unknown to myself. Tender breast, cell of patience. Tentative tenderness, as cells divide.

Heap of hourglass sand. Mind merely prickles, pecks at.

I entrust my sleep to the ocean I hear out each window.

TO SEE WHAT'S THERE

Plastic owl perched
on a baseball fence
in the park
     your dark
wings then flew

*

Sonoma moonrise
full tomorrow   sun burns red
   against the ridge
    Cross the bridge
slow fog engulfed

SEA SO CALM WE DO NOT NOTE THE TIDE

You are the only noun to appear like a shell, moth, flower of five unequal petals, honeyed as sweet pea. Itch to drink milky black tea, bitter pale.

So we recognize a verse known by heart where we never expected it to be.

You are the small rain, small beer, little beer glass, lazy errand boy.

I relish the skin of a caramel custard, the din when I have a good seat. But you are morning's nagging question, the query I muzzle where I pasture that prancing wish.

O palest glistening chrysalis green.

NEWS KNOWN
SOONER ABROAD

The doctor saw first. Gelled wand inside me. Small, she said. There's a heartbeat. Slow. Too slow. Dragged a measure across the screen. Too small.

Sent home to wait. Smother me soft in baby's breath and butter muslin. Let fall small money to ripple the fountain. Climb the hill.

Any creature with the head of a man will face you differently. Bind the book of autumn, ember-leafed difficulty. Pea coat in the closet, embarrassed, left diffidently.

Can a heartbeat quicken? Mismeasured, I bargained, unmeasured, immeasurable.

Any foreign city can be a mellifluous note.

The true sky was grey.

AN EMPTY MEASURE IN MUSIC

That the dead could linger. Measure to the first knuckle of my littlest finger. Hand-worked guipure, light wool for a shawl. My body a shroud, lost all, lost all. Flicker, spark, and softest fall.

I count the beats in stillness.

Slattern with cups and spoons and days, I wish for fields of thorns, of waves. Carve out covetousness to leave only longing. Desire without envy, eyeless blinding. Bed of tangled leaves, a useless binding. Turn and leave this waste uncrossed.

I wait to lose you, already lost.

FOR RESPITE

Despite the thought
the blood the red
                    leaves
            red leaves feeling
leaves
for a time

LIKE THE NATIVE TONGUE THE VANQUISHED

Repeat. Quince against my window, nenuphar by the stepping-stone.

Remember the home you will not see again. Repeat the words as time distorts them. Child.

Rosy quinces, coincidental roses.

A choice to wait or scrape. Dilated and awake. Curette. Body forced past its margins. Cold sweat and bile. Chilled.

Sticky spot they scrubbed too tentatively. Retained products of conception, the form will later read.

I chose this. Spring that bristles my jurisdiction, elasticity that drives my domain. Pussy willow twig tapping the skylight above my childhood bed.

Unmeasured pressures have changed the dimensions of that feeling. Hills and valleys in relief. The shore on strike.

SWEET TEA

A single changed event would mean a different child
Unfurling inside where that heart grew and stilled,
So each small spoilage, broken ankle, burnt apple caramel,
I decide to read as choreography, what led to this.
As fog spilled over the basin of the hill, I chilled
My voice to blue raspberry ice, artificial and distant,
Described dates, days, ways I bled in flush and clot.
Now bathysphere, I house a slow advance. Brain and bone.
Stretched seams silvering. Your red world of fish
Sounds, burbling. I sing; you hiccup—lungs growing
Under skin that rises, ripples when your synapse
Fires. Sweet tea flutters you, swimming in sugar water.
Sometimes still for hours, I prod, body, awaken:
This is mine and mine and yours under, it's you.

TO LIVE WITH WEATHER

Sugar shot plum bursts
jam tomorrow
                fog gusts
        Chill August
San Francisco
time unspun

*

Diminished lake
this lovely sun
has wronged
        songs
echo dread and dry

I COULD NOT ASK
OTHER FLOWERS

Today multiplied.

A layered wealth of strata along the sloped face of the work. Ankle bone, wind-blown grain, suck of honeysuckle, cell of honeycomb.

Approach the hedgerow with reverence due a rood loft (consent, oh Lord, to bless). Spade in hand, cleave what knotted. 1 am of the same stripe as she who cries into the thorned canopy. 1 follow her gaze to the engraved steeple, bricked with birds' nests.

Talus, you were broken before, alveolus, breathe honeyed air and speak the landscape of this body. Thoughts pile up, bent, twined, twisted as flowers.

CIRCUMSTANCES LEGIBLE BEHIND THIS WINDOW

What is raw in me again, burst blister, lamb's lettuce.

Hang on syllables, frivolous, drowsing. All modifiers are contagious. Complacent. Glowing. All modifiers slip me in the direction of the sea.

Without the residue of fixed habits, I loosen my gauge to make sweet the absences. Lace is made of holes. Like a bassinet on a lower step, my hum rocks side to side. Water diminishes in the basin as the days grow drier. I say guard and mean keep.

AGAINST WHAT DIMINISHES

Made smaller
by rejection
reduced
      like vinegar
            stronger
sweeter

TAKE SEASON AND WEATHER AS A FRAME

Events occurred against you.

Baited hook, primed pump, path that leads to every other path I no longer remember. How at every bend, I imagined you beyond. Exercise heart's agility to quicken.

Vine I learned to cut, wine I did not drink. Evening's entertainment, slow blur politely clung to. In tomorrow's cursive, all equivocating cheer of epistolary.

I told a woman. Behind her, photographs of her grown daughters. She said back in Egypt her belly grew hard, how strangers still reached a hand to touch what stilled.

Move this flame from my sleeve.

Call of some bird drowned out by the question. I would not name what I could not see.

SKEIN OF RED CASHMERE

Already too late, my friend said, I will take steps to prevent it.

Twelve languid days, her body was obscured. Listless arms by shadow veiled.

Heedless, can I say without bitterness? Friend, did you imagine a moment's soft hum under apple blossoms?

Tender bud, unbecoming. Now nebula, the mildest haunting.

Burn stars that this bruise, gift refused, come again propitious.

So we are left to carve away all surfeit till the figure gleams. Yet leave some rock unpolished. Ivy binds along the cliff.

THE BEAUTY OF BEINGS UNLIKE THAT OF OBJECTS

Both knowing how I wanted, even broken, what she hated to throw away, we wrote daily. Fountain pen, bitter ink, tentacle across this letter. Mooring cable, tell what came next.

Enough, she says. Let breathing be enough today. A reflection, alien as if I'd placed myself in the framed vision of a doe.

Odds against the imperfect. In comfort, every friend's mother says spared.

I could not say I had a daughter. I had a syndrome, missing chromosomes nature mostly culls. A colleague tells me she studies what for me was a sentence.

I had that, I answer. Lost it. Her.

For weeks, opacity staved back the Norns. Morning an array, a rain. One hand measures what the eddy reclaims. Windfall, a gift of losing.

Not every godsend is a bargain. Lucky break of the last elm branch. Friend, we walked the beach bleeding, spoke and smiled through that red.

TO ACCEPT COMFORT

Baby bathes
My lip bruised
from his hard crown
          Lean down
his palm along my cheek
repeating "gentle"
hurts a little

A SICKNESS DOES NOT RESEMBLE

We suffer crossing the lintel. Wash and walk the body that has failed you. Sweat and wash the sweat. Feed her almond butter rice cakes.

Care for this body as if she were the child you wanted.

Grapefruit's bitter pith.

Tenderness lingers on, bedridden. Boil water, sip linden blossoms. A manicure varnishes the dolor. Late morning, smooth an acorn. Run a finger along the piping of your bonnet.

Beneath a basswood tree, turn briefly to emigrate for parts of yourself still a stranger.

What we call by another name, we live differently. This linden bower my cell. This clump of cells my love. We grasp what's mutable.

Things we know, we hold. So ask. Body, are you unfaithful while you dip a biscuit in a teacup?

I called the nurse only when the clots stretched me, tough meat. Whose body, I asked. Heard hard hurt blood left too long.

TO GUIDE THE KNIFE

Anxiety   dark spot
   on peach blush
                  carve it out
                  the doubt
   it runs straight through

BRUISED PEACHES

We measure days in peaches, bruises, livid, lose the keys,
Find them days later in the dirty laundry. What is habit
That it wakes me up to effort? I cook but don't dust, read
In bed, wash the sheets occasionally. Eat the peaches
Before they mold, wear wool socks against a cold July.
My signature slants "O" to a recognizable angle—what is
Unnoticed is unchanging; the B negative of my blood, unchecked,
Will reject babies that could have poisoned me in another age.
Might effort tilt the ratios of my articles, definite stamp of
All I've heard and hardened indefinite in what I make. A child is
Variable flung from the cells, being, substance-sewn
Self. In coming hours, a turn, determined angle, harkening,
Effortless. Biology wakes me to that cry. Subterranean
Singing through the fabric, thin-spread-thing, I am still here.

IN THE EXHAUSTION OF CARE

Night vomit
hot bath you say
colder than I'd rather
                    I lather
half your hair

*

4am   careful
I cough into
            the pillow
            still you
cry

*

Small hands all day
body unsovereign
How deep is patience
            mealy peaches
sweet thing

*

Sleep at last
rejected breast
                my unconsoled
leaked milk now cold
against my wrist

AGAINST REACTION

Make a study of patience
       Lift him shrieking from the bath
Let hands tell only tenderness
       Let him   through childhood's wilderness
know limit free of anger

EVOKE THE FOREST WHERE A LAIR IS HID

With a single leafy branch of palisander.

Call a tree ardent when it produces more leaves than fruit. Show me to approach with open hands. Silk scarf tossed over a bare shoulder.

But I am veteran of the perverse wish to tear the new green growth from the pine tree. Only at night, the goodly mouth of my candle sparks a face in you. Resin scent lingers.

The wall we build blinds our house in one eye.

MOON, WITHOUT POSSIBLE APPROACH

Did friends neglect me because they had everything I wished? Kept a waiting room in flowers. Blue of winter afternoon pressed against the windows. Cheek cooled against condensation. I slept the sleep I had no relish for while they paced through colic.

Rejoicing covers me with pastry; I am pinched.

Easy confidence of strangers at dinners. Blushing announcements are not punished for their fearlessness. And why should they be.

One form listed diagnosis: spontaneous aborter. Rage at who names a body.

Most people experience this as a loss, the first doctor said.

I am fond of a hedge at this hour. Find a cobalt marble, smooth bone I plucked from a stone wall, gritty silt, in the pocket of last year's jacket. Dizzy clustered asters, steep path.

Frock coat of discretion. Dovecote small shelter in a rain storm. Blood wet white feathers mired.

Distant diminishing glow.

TYRANNY OF THE PARTICULAR

Up late, my husband eats Raisin Bran from an empty ice cream quart. I bleed with daily dull red clotting. No one washes the dishes.

Here, let's admire an orchid, that conspicuous fringed lip called cattleya. I am yours where the snipped bud engraves jasper. Sea of leaves, carpet of pebbles.

Any word can be an elevated bridge leading into fog. What's beyond, obscured. Yet transport.

My friend says any day now. Instrumentalist for whom the moment has not yet arrived to execute her part. At her feet a trunk of folded cotton. Layette I too would prepare.

Neglected succulents strain in tangles against a window I wander past. Learn to savor blind-spots, revelation infinitely delayed.

How a hart inhabits the stagger. How adamant contains a piece of rock.

OUR KNOWLEDGE OF FACES

Days became known. Further acquaintance worked like subtraction, marking paths of imagination I could no longer follow. Trimmed fingernails, a heap of gold grubby crescents no longer part of me. Cauterized lost hours. Avoided artifacts of that hope. Softest alpaca two-ply.

Pacifier.

Campfires, incarnadine embers, my habit of holding a cup of tea on my lap. Talking late, his doubts of the incarnation, my librettos of chaff. Then he touched me.

Without intention, returned to what had been enough. More. Hand on my thigh. Soft stroke demands the pained part feel pleasure.

In the present of this room, we don't speak of how time passes.

How could I walk if it were only me that grieved it? We carry risk unevenly. But we both carry it.

A time comes when I can't see a future different from the past. Still, I will repeat it.

He decides it is enough to know something "just because." In exchange, I give him the sun-warmed side of the melon.

TO SEE BOTH SIDES

Ungentle elbow
against her   still
        he bites
        the grape
and feeds his sister half

FOR THE JOY OF SPECIFICITY

My son says
give me
      as many peas
      as a wolf has teeth
and so I do   forty-two

WE REQUIRE THE RISK
OF IMPOSSIBILITY

Everything I don't understand this evening is blooming.

The paths, perfect and separate halves of a pear, lead past riparian glades, near a tangle of duckweed and periwinkle.

As if I could catch a brill from the pump trough or invent some bearded lettuce. Place a salamander near the sweetly balsamic impatiens.

First spring shower still cousin to the snow. Still, some sprout. Let weeds grow.

Unless I sit under the shade of a poplar, pluck with my fingers chestnut, puffball, bold whirligig of maple, I doubt.

Vetch blossom pollen. Sweet sap of the apiary. I forget a scourge can be a literal slap.

AWAITING

My attention's fixed, but you're distant by necessity, all color muted. Vouchsafe that harm pass me over.

Allocate a little yellow, a gradually chronic underbelly, a stabbing at the slightest breeze.

Canary, come to me like your yellow, all suddenness. In the small lagoon of my drifting ear, a brightening.

TO RECALL THAT SOUND

His macaw chirps
resonate the banjo
He bites the jam spoon
        jams typewriter keys
spooning
        flips and claws

RITES DEMANDED

After heavy rains, a river shifts from its course. Unformed water flows down an offered slope. A smooth stone in my mouth. Sleep another hour.

Awake. Tremble in the breeze like wheat.

Nothing languid in this concentration. Taste salt on the lip, apprehend a wicker basket as a possible sign of presence.

Take up shears. Slice hollow husks of lilac. Shell, hull, musk of riverbank. Blanket, dwell, shade of lichen-light.

Unharnessed tongue, that immeasurable clavier, almost entirely unknown.

AGAINST CHOKING

I find a sprig of thyme
lodged in the back corner
of his mouth   gummed
            and pungent
hazards where he crawls

*

Late she coughs awake
voluptuous milk mouth
            eyes shut   rapt
I feel the let-down   lie trapped
recall the paperclip my finger found

TO BE THE CLIFF WAVES
BREAK AGAINST

My son hits me
no pain all gesture
then red   wrung
            tear-stung
demands embrace

*

Clutching brother's alligator
my daughter tests anger
red-faced holler
            she's smaller
yells louder

*

Enough I say   In anger
we seek comfort and reject it
            rage impelled
he wants to be held
but not touched

TO LOVE WHAT'S BEEN USED

Sun-screen slick
child still fits
        lifts muddy fist
against a pale near-empty breast

MOON IN DAYLIGHT

A less insistent presence. Call it a lingering.

In the tempest, once the sea has been sufficiently swollen, it will spill.

And perhaps each being is destroyed when we cease to see her, her next appearance a new creation. So we abandon even ourselves in sleep.

Once the sea has been sufficiently buffeted, it will surge.

On a ship, I look for the indent of an open-necked coastline, edged with ribbons of pale light. In travel, for the pleasure of measuring the difference between departure and arrival as profound.

In remaining, I look to increase.

In the struggle to put myself in the path of new accidents, all intention goes to waste.

Return gently, first frost, pale hailstones, I look for you.

But I no longer speak it.

RUBIES, SOAP, AND BRONZE

Each word singly gives me an earful, but I'm unsure who suffers from complaints of the bladder, who searches for columbines in the bower.

A story hangs from its end. A translation, the present carries multiples.

I submit three job applications, sing the children to bed, drink a beer in the bath.

We'll move next year. Somewhere. Not that job, not there. It's easier to tell myself I was never that person. Easier to accept a bribe in a foreign tongue from a woman draped in venomous flowers. All day I saw the loss in blossom, the end in friend. I stay to dig through such layers of silt.

The pot left on the back burner keeps vigil, the night-light keeps vigil.

IN UNCERTAINTY

Walking through city rain
so my son can sing carols
imagining prairie
            his hair
wet as mine

*

Sympathy invites tears
my body leaks them
Walk past palms   next year
            not here
what other paths   what trees?

TO RELINQUISH THE STORY

Give the feeling
          infinite space
Say here rises the moon
of my worries   untuned
dark sea

of my exhaustion
Let it last forever
          A child plumbs this font
          says I will *never* want
to wear pajamas

OUR MEMORIES REST
OUTSIDE OURSELVES

Portholes of thick glass refract spires. I choose a seat by the fire, the violet tulips, the wisteria window.

When you think of setting, consider a gem that fell out. Locate a ring on the hand. I can't see her face, the ringing phone. Locate her voice in a room. A sound in the phrase. Face the difficulty of knowing how deeply our words penetrate the reality of others.

Unexpected vernal shames the hawthorn to bloom unrest. Iridescent ammonite, her voice an index fossil of what I felt. She tells me how trapped blood pained tender held too tight by her body.

Speak into the silence.

My baby babbles like a fountain. Kiss the salt flower.

TO ACKNOWLEDGE DAMAGE

Stirring damsons
steam and garnet
a friend's sudden rupture
            how suture
that longing to cradle

*

One-year
fearless she stumbles
top lip tooth-cut
        her suck
mingles milk and blood

UMBILICAL

Blue umbilical pulse to cut, my last placenta
Stuck, the doctor scrubbed elbow-deep, that flesh
Suddenly neither of us, excess, would rot inside me.
I held him, purple still and scrawny, bawling.
Hot blankets, shivering, sweat-wracked, hormone high—
What is in the body, yours, mind, all mouth? We are
Our parts, not a self apart, grow new ancillaries, collaborate
On blood. My son nears three now, swipes and taps
Glass-faced watch-hands, asks if the umbilicus plugs
Into the wall. Charged up on Coca-Cola, wails, "hard peaches
Are my favorite." He wants what's unripe. I slice and macerate
With sweet and salt and mint, tired now beyond cheek's fuzz
And bloom. New one, I made you a room inside my mind.
Still you'll split my skin to quit me.

NOTHING IN THE BOOK
OR IN THE STONE

Doorkeeper, all this dross. At the train station on the way to an evening. First wood-fire smoke in the air. Skirt hem on which I stitch your name. Vocables of the branch line, music for which silent reading is not sufficient.

How gradually, how repeatedly. How reassurance made wasps' nests between slow, then absent, heartbeats.

She tells me of a sudden seam of red.

A wasp hovers over a family of grasses. Unlike the bee who stings only once.

Some days the rains simply drip-drop, pit-pat.

On a morning when time begins again, I address a letter to the house you no longer inhabit.

In the autonomy of each hour, the remove of a nightingale.

TO MEASURE

Stay he says
a tiny tiny bit
I think I'll count three trains
four   five   what remains
          of awareness
spent listening   subsides

FOR PERMISSION TO GO

Morning her chirp
through the door
I leave shut
            no kindness to greet
and leave

FLAWS PARTICULAR TO EACH

A church is built ship and means to sail. A packed chancel shoals supplications. I make demands. The apse, the abscess, how both contain. Turn to think of other pleas refused.

Like barrel vaults in parallel, let these outward reaching aches sustain. Lean then against another. Incline.

Thine ear.

Purl and dream of the ceremonially sheared vicuña. Every four years, a warm and supple fabric. Wild ancestor of the alpaca, girl in the golden coat.

Swollen after scraping. Only showers, no bathing.

Memory, notebook no larger than a matchbook. Sleep, shop of old medals and lapis paperweights engraved with anchors.

Rain, a clean insistence, grain of salt, treacherous lullaby.

IN SLEEPLESSNESS

Baby cries no lullabies
can calm   I pace
the floorboards creak
        I sway   they squeak
Her still stern face listening

BY GIFT, PURCHASE, CAPTURE, OR INHERITANCE

A daffodil, a silken thread. Out-dated ring, a history of encounters. I pluck out her stone.

At my age, mother to four. Flushing, she pinched a nerve in my father's elbow. Some native to that place shape my eyes. Both sides passed down, what can I claim.

Another grandmother approached the wasps' nest with hinged tea strainer and boiling water, sewed glow-worms for three daughters. Her husband strung a loom with rough wool.

Moths found last winter's sweaters. Withered basil, each apartment dims. Glimmer. I speak a language no known mother tongued.

Visit a fortress near Urbino. Examine the embrasure. Who preceded me alive then. Beaches of Mumbles Head, woods of Tennessee. I do not know what they built. Only clouds move the same.

Turn west to face the fields, acquire lack.

FOR WHAT FINGERS TOUCH

Knuckle prickles
purl then pick
    rough twig or grass
  a sheep brushed past
now shorn   spun yarn

*

We wind the wool
small son spins slow
         let baby sleep
       pinch here to keep
the tension steady

CREATING WHAT WE NAME

I sing-song back the slightest blossoming, let it echo against the flagstones, now present.

This running hem on the wrong side is felt, finger caressed. Rub in lanolin. Worry cuticles. Felt fabric, boiled wool. Cut with shears, a pleasing snick. Evening, cut with soda water. Sheer bloody-mindedness outlasts bitter blooms.

Mirabilis. Blood-seeping.

Some word we lost in the din of the hunt in the heat of the day.

My look of concentration always a frown as I remove seeds from a melon. Sonorous zither, drop of lemon.

LOCKED IN THE PRESENT

Dust motes beneath the trellis sieve evening light. I make jam from the pale unripe apricots of early June.

Sound flutters thought into smooth uneven heaps. Thinking through opacity's curve. Furrows undisturbed, waver, aver.

Hand held in ice water.

I wish not only to cease, but to cease wishing. Apply sugar, heat, and time.

Evacuated day, mere surplus, drill the fingering to a minor chord.

Look close enough to say Madonna with Siskin, close enough to see the tied-cloth pacifier.

CLOISTER OF HABITS

Flowers know better what to make of seeds than my body.

Make a safe seclusion of repeated actions. Wake early, walk lightly.

Make a soup for consumptives, trust the wrong roots. Sup on larks' tongue. Turn glassy-eyed, glossy as a worm-eaten apple's fair side.

Bloom of health, leaking clot. Landscape of days, *Dracula* and lace.

Misericord. Here again the hawthorn. Sleep another hour, eyes sealed against colored flame.

Some say to name them. I will not.

IN UNBEARABLE TRANSIENCE

Dark morning awake
before my daughter
early dusk   my son lies still
Against day's rush
            this hush
breathing soft the sleep I hold

TO ACKNOWLEDGE RESEMBLANCE

Baby wants
the onion I'm peeling
says "apple"   reaches
                    Each name
an object's round moon

*

Two years old
he thinks mirrors
are pictures
            face flickers
to grimace

FOR CURIOSITY

Heavy hollow branch he thumped
on playground paving
         and pill bugs
      spilled
so many wriggling

TO RETURN TO THE BODY

From solitary sleep
awake
                    slow ripples
slack mouth on my nipple
pinch of small teeth

*

Her thread twirls pain
blooms along my brow
                    eyes tear
                    Hold here
scent of onion I peeled

ACACIA STREET OF APPARITIONS

I would like for once to be very wrong. Onion tears are prettiest.

The swamp bears its lack of tides bitterly—we have not left salt behind.

Show devotion to the moon's determination. Light a votive to a tree with velvet eyes of a beast.

Bowing branches inscribe a shadow lyric, braid of eclogues against the dim.

As if l could stop expecting long enough to frolic in a clearing. Auspicious day for reading something into the oak tree.

IN THE SPIRIT OF THE TRANSITORY

We make lasting decisions.

Tomorrow no longer exterior and vast, as I'd feverishly expected, but a new point of departure for desiring more.

If I had a single word for vague desire. If I thought a sailboat wore a veil. If I could leave it alone.

A packed trunk trails crumpled petals once damp. Substitute the opacity of sounds for the transparence of ideas. My memory is cross-hatched with words, voice a pale blue wash of watercolor.

I keep a weather eye on your shrugging shoulders. Face an empty shoreline at low tide.

TO BE THE STORY'S
TIRED MAKER

Toy boats   the sink over-flooding
sop up sodden towels
water hot against cold hands
        no heat I say no
                story   by tree glow
relenting   speak that tired love   so the wolf

FOR THE MOUTH

Clapped hands
when he saw the carousel
rode the retriever   caroused
                Parasol and varnish
doubt the sound
        intention mulls it

ELIMINATE THE DISTANCE

In late summer, step over the frame of sliding windows into the quiet dining room. Evening light permits it. Quit the swarm along the embankment to stand silent as a flush hinge.

Day devours breath. Count three and know it.

What is in your mouth upon waking? A tongue is word and taste. Lemon. Meander. You will speak today.

On each panel of the altarpiece, whose human hand cut leaves, stars, and fishes?

How to see ruins as something someone else has broken or abandoned, though I love the grass between pillars as I love the eucalyptus shedding bark. A courtyard whole, a swell of music, voices raised in prayer.

Turn the creaking hand-crank of a darkened well. Wait for uncertain water.

Melon.

Leander.

THREE-HOUR LABOR

Waters ruptured with a crochet hook when Pitocin
Did nothing. If I can still read, it's not happening.
I finish *Sunshine*, start another book. Screen blips
Regular, inefficacious, on the clock, I don't want
Her cut out of me. Morning, pacing (leaking, weeping)
This echo chamber, her chambered-heart pulsing
Enclosed—she's inside still and I'm locked
In the sound of her blood. Redoubled dose,
Too fast to saturate, at last answers, enough,
Too much. Now hum into the pause
Till no pause comes. Still plugged in, hands clench,
Clutch, IV bleats complaint at the kinked tube,
But I can't connect sound with act. Surrounded,
Self in the clench of muscle, burning with her.

TO NO LONGER SUFFER
FROM THEM

We must know our dreams entirely.

Travel to a foggy place. Eat buckwheat crepes. Use old words to tell of what is new.

You are a metonymy along the horizon. I, all unstitched rambling. I will knit a breastplate. I will knit a shoulder cape. A dickey and a shawl beside spring's prickling blossoms.

Between two shores, a ford, again becalmed, a spur.

TO ACCEPT DAILINESS

Evening fruit flies hover over
split banana legs tomato
                    Wash more dishes
                    take down fish skin
carrot tops cucumber peelings

overflowing diapers papers
Little daughter drops cucumber
                    warm bath for you
                    brand new left shoe
missing already

IN REPEATED ACTION

Scarlet runners'
salt–foam simmer
windows steam of sleep
       stir

  *

Sheets of egg and flour
thin through repetition
          soft against my thumb
          So let thoughts come
Knit the silk the moths ignore

TO BE ALONE OR APPEAR
TO DESIRE IT

The tight-closed purple peonies never opened. I kept changing their murky water.

Cabinets of ebony so dense they sink under waves. I thought ebony violent as ivory. A part cut off. Mary in *The Secret Garden* plays with tiny ivory elephants. So violence carves a replica of what it breaks. Piano sharps, dark against the ear.

Lace, first frost, visits iron work, my patience, thin traveling thread. Here silk wears ragged.

A millstone is a burden only when no one thinks where flour comes from. Carry hope like a weight.

YOU RECOGNIZE YOUR ROSES

I hoped for a botanical pardon, that filament of particular to notice.

Monkey puzzle tree.

Venerate the pale spur of the young plant. Cradle tea cups in chilly palms. Do hours count only when we cast a shadow?

Brightness on the train of a gown. Forgotten pickax against a root. Pomelo we squeeze and leave the pulp. Thin tare won't wash out.

So the wooden bowl became the begging bowl.

Lift emptiness.

Her head heavy now on my shoulder. Drink cold tea from a glass jar, work fiddling stitches in purple silk.

IF PLEASURE CONTRACTS
WITH CERTITUDE

Recall tomorrow's chance of sleet.

A mushroom left on a sheet of paper overnight releases its spores.

Rub beeswax block crayon blue over veined leaf. Stamp a slum of bloom with cut core of celery.

Watch pink sugar-water thicken, sticky, crystalize. Pierce with thumbnail the perfumed navel of a clementine.

Swim against the waves, held by what resists you.

Tousled poppies cling to jagged rock. Paltry red above the dusking crash, twilight makes you only fingers' silk.

Evening its own consolation. Life annuity of stars without constellation.

DREAM OF HATCHING CHICKENS

Alive, dead, membrane peeling, loose skin, unfeathered
Horror, then peeping, hungry, gold grey fluff. In April
Fall's frost-blighted apples still clung to the branch.
Now June, all day the bees, my mother's straining lungs.
Both alive and dead, chicks hatched in boxes I'd forgotten,
Unfed in the dark. To make a shape of the pieces
Betrays them. Do it anyway. My son tells me chicks hatch
In 21 to 28 days. My blood comes early, inconvenience now,
Not pain. To braid grasses, to bend green sprigs into a wreath.
Here, I'm holding this circle for you. A cello around the corner
Wars with a violin down the hall. I open the door to let them in.
Outside are branches thick with young apples. Making makes
More, hatches another, warm, peeping, hungry.
Don't save anything for later.

AMULET

Little daughter Vesper
be somber cedar incense
be tart like citrus

ACKNOWLEDGMENTS

Poems from this collection, at times in quite different states of revision, have appeared in the chapbooks *Vesper Vigil* (above/ground 2016), *The Loss Letters* (Dusie Press 2010), *Scaffolding* (Dusie Press 2009), and *Like the Native Tongue the Vanquished* (Cannibal Books 2008), as well as in the following journals: *IIII*, *About Place*, *Bennington Review*, *Calaveras*, *CapGun*, *The Concher*, *The Cultural Society*, *Denver Quarterly*, *Fact Simile*, *Forklift Ohio*, *Fou*, *Foursquare*, *Grist*, *Guest*, *The Laurel Review*, *Left Facing Bird*, *LIT*, *Little Red Leaves*, *Mary*, *Matchbook Magazine*, *Mississippi Review*, *The New Yinzer*, *No Tell Motel*, *The Ocean State Review*, *Potash Hill*, *The Rumpus*, *Sixth Finch*, *Tarpaulin Sky*, *the tiny*, *Tinfish*, *Touch the Donkey*, *Typo*, *We Are So Happy to Know Something*, and *Xavier*. Warm thanks to the editors and staffs of these publications, especially Matthew Henriksen, Susana Gardner, and rob mclennan.

Thanks to Jessica Fisher and Megan Gravendyk-Estrella for choosing this book for the Hillary Gravendyk Prize.

Many of these poems began with reading Proust in French, which I read well but not perfectly, in search of words I did not know and could not make a confident guess at. I used these words, my guesses based on context, strange collisions, their etymology, French dictionary references (sometimes only to the Proustian sentence in which I'd encountered them), and the guts of my beloved OED for drafting material. While much of what this process generated has been trimmed away in revisions, I've gratefully retained some plants, some syntax, some atmosphere, and many titles.

Thanks to Caleb, Vesper, and Owen, for time to write and love to inscribe. Thanks to my parents, Matthew and Theresa, and my sister, Sophie, for holding me through all of it.

Thanks to my poetry and poetics teachers, Forrest Gander, C.D. Wright, Thalia Field, Catherine Imbriglio, Keith Waldrop, Robert Creeley, Roland Greene, Margaret Cohen, Sepp Gumbrecht, Ben Lerner, Réda Bensmaia, Susan Bernstein, Marjorie Welish, Mary Ann Allegretto, Tim Joy, and all the others beyond the classroom.

Thanks to Ming Holden, Leila K. Norako, and Lucy Alford, poetry exchange collaborators and early readers of many of the first seeds and sprouts of this book.

Thanks to Rusty Morrison for a keenly insightful read-through that helped me rethink everything.

Gratitude and love to Lynn Xu, Kate Schapira, Caroline Whitbeck, and Michael Tod Edgerton, my first companions in thinking deeply about poems and looking up animals on petfinder.com. You're still the editing angels in my ear (and sometimes for real on the phone). So kind and so smart. Lucky me.

Big love to Bridget Whearty, Hannah Hudson, Becky Richardson, and Jill Hess, the world's best dissertation writing group. Thanks for continuing to read what I sent you when it became poems instead of dissertation chapters. I can't imagine my writing life without our long-distance Pomodoro writing and late-night texts. RT forever!

Thanks to my correspondents and inspirations: Anna Henderson, Kate Clark, Jessalynn Gale, Jessica Weare, Kjerstin Gruys, Tom Andes, Adam Clay, Angela Beccera Vidergar, Mattia Acetoso, Elizabeth McBreen, Jessica Smith, Cynthia Arrieu-King, MC Hyland, Camille Guthrie, Danielle Pafunda, Rage Hezekiah, K. Lorraine Graham, Jen Tynes, Jasmine Kitses, Sara Renee Marshall, Ginger Ko, Jules Cohen, and so many more.

Thanks to everyone I've taught in company with, especially Adam Johnson, Blakey Vermeule, Gabriella Safran, Amy Beecher, Jean O'Hara, Amer Latif, John Sheehy, and Gloria Biamonte. I've learned so much from you.

Thanks to my students, especially Marie Creel, Anna Morrissey, Thomas Nuhfer, Maya Faerstein-Weiss, Adeel Sultan, Em Hexe, Catherine Canann, Eli Douglas, Lucy Johnston, Adara Miter, Sam Amber, Noah Strauss-Jenkins, Raf Cornel, Roan Lee-Plunket, Brooke Evans, Hannah McGowan, Daniel Medeiros, Kristen Thompson, and Nora Wooden. Getting to talk about books and poems and feelings and metaphors and line-breaks and ideas and all of it with each of you has been the dream. Seriously.

Bronwen Tate is an Assistant Professor of Teaching in the
School of Creative Writing at the University of British
Columbia in Vancouver, BC. A citizen of the Chickasaw
Nation, Bronwen earned an MFA in Literary Arts from
Brown University and a PhD in Comparative Literature
from Stanford University. She is the author of several poetry
chapbooks, and her poems and essays have appeared in
publications including *Bennington Review, Denver Quarterly,
CV2, The Rumpus, Journal of Modern Literature*, and the MLA
volume *Options for Teaching Modernist Women's Writing in
English*. Her work has been supported by Stanford's DARE
(Diversifying Academia Recruiting Excellence) Dissertation
Fellowship, as well as by fellowships from the Stanford
Humanities Center and Vermont Studio Center. Read more of
her work or get in touch at www.bronwentate.com.

ABOUT THE HILLARY GRAVENDYK PRIZE

The Hillary Gravendyk Prize is an open poetry book competition published by Inlandia Institute for all writers regardless of the number of previously published poetry collections.

HILLARY GRAVENDYK (1979-2014) was a beloved poet living and teaching in Southern California's "Inland Empire" region. She wrote the acclaimed poetry book, *HARM* from Omnidawn Publishing (2012) and the posthumously published *The Soluble Hour* (Omnidawn, 2017) and *Unlikely Conditions* (1913 Press, 2017, with Cynthia Arrieu-King) as well as the poetry chapbook *The Naturalist* (Anchiote Press, 2008).. A native of Washington State, she was an admired Assistant Professor of English at Pomona College in Claremont, CA. Her poetry has appeared widely in journals such as *American Letters & Commentary, The Bellingham Review, The Colorado Review, The Eleventh Muse, Fourteen Hills, MARY, 1913: A Journal of Forms, Octopus Magazine, Tarpaulin Sky* and *Sugar House Review*. She was awarded a 2015 Pushcart Prize for her poem "Your Ghost," which appeared in the Pushcart Prize Anthology. She leaves behind many devoted colleagues, friends, family and beautiful poems. Hillary Gravendyk passed away on May 10, 2014 after a long illness. This contest has been established in her memory.

ABOUT INLANDIA INSTITUTE

Inlandia Institute is a regional non-profit and literary center. We seek to bring focus to the richness of the literary enterprise that has existed in this region for ages. The mission of the Inlandia Institute is to recognize, support, and expand literary activity in all of its forms in Inland Southern California by publishing books and sponsoring programs that deepen people's awareness, understanding, and appreciation of this unique, complex and creatively vibrant region.

The Institute publishes books, presents free public literary and cultural programming, provides in-school and after school enrichment programs for children and youth, holds free creative writing workshops for teens and adults, and boot camp intensives. In addition, every two years, the Inlandia Institute appoints a distinguished jury panel from outside of the region to name an Inlandia Literary Laureate who serves as an ambassador for the Inlandia Institute, promoting literature, creative literacy, and community. Laureates to date include Susan Straight (2010-2012), Gayle Brandeis (2012-2014), Juan Delgado (2014-2016), Nikia Chaney (2016-2018), and Rachelle Cruz (2018-2020).

To learn more about the Inlandia Institute, please visit our website at www.InlandiaInstitute.org.

OTHER HILLARY GRAVENDYK PRIZE BOOKS

Remyth: A Postmodern Ritual by Adam D. Martinez
Winner of the 2019 Regional Hillary Gravendyk Prize

Former Possessions of the Spanish Empire by Michelle Peñaloza
Winner of the 2018 National Hillary Gravendyk Prize

All the Emergency-Type Structures by Elizabeth Cantwell
Winner of the 2018 Regional Hillary Gravendyk Prize

Our Bruises Kept Singing Purple by Malcolm Friend
Winner of the 2017 National Hillary Gravendyk Prize

Traces of a Fifth Column by Marco Maisto
Winner of the 2016 National Hillary Gravendyk Prize

God's Will for Monsters by Rachelle Cruz
Winner of the 2016 Regional Hillary Gravendyk Prize
Winner of a 2018 American Book Award

Map of an Onion by Kenji C. Liu
Winner of the 2015 National Hillary Gravendyk Prize

All Things Lose Thousands of Times by Angela Peñaredondo
Winner of the 2015 Regional Hillary Gravendyk Prize